A Tourists Guide

to European Plumbing

CONTINENTAL CANS ETC,

by

PERRIN C. MILLER

and

RUTH WILLOCK

drawings by

MILDA VIZBAR

DEDICATION

To our excellent hosts and worthy friends throughout Europe, this frivolous effort, produced in the spirit of raillery rather than ridicule, is dutifully dedicated.

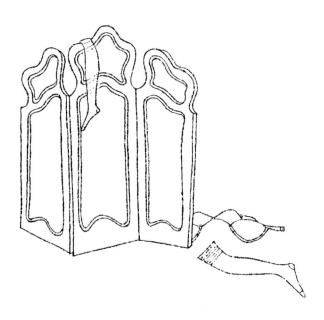

INTRODUCTION

Remember ... if you are taking yourself to Europe it is partly because Europe is different. Therein lies much of its charm. Some strange customs, some strange facilities and some strange signs. These latter are to be strictly observed. Mr. Sydney Clark, world traveller, has graciously supplied us with a transcript of one of the important ones (taken from the toilet room of a continental train):

> When the fact does not vest the character
> of voluntary damage if the transgressor
> declares himself ready to make an oblation
> equal to the minimum of the fines over and
> above the eventual damages the agent receives
> the sum and gives a receipt. The oblation
> extinguishes the penal action.

Please be governed accordingly.

PLUMBING TERMS

a lexicon for the timid traveller

DAMES.................*What else?*

MESDAMES............*Seen in better places*

HOMMES................*Gents*

MESSIEURS............*Ditto in better places*

DAMEN.................*Teutonic version of Dames*

HERREN................*Ditto of Gents*

DONNE..................*Italian version of Dames*

UOMINI.................*Ditto of Gents*

SIGNORE..............*High Class Dames*

SIGNORI...............*Ditto of Gents*

LAVABO................*Wash hand stand (trans. from the French)*

DOUCHE...............*Shower. Everyone knows that.*

DOCCIA................*Ditto in Italian*

W. C....................*One for all, all for one.*
Originally, water closet.

BIDET...................*Controversial item. See asterisk, page 36.*

PISSOIR................*For the gents, hommes, herren, uomini, etc.*

BAGNI di PIEDI...*Wonderful after a day on the cobbles.*

LE STAND-BY.......*Pot de chambre. So?*

There are more?

9

LE STANDBY, ON LOCATION...

While belonging to a period,

LE STAND-BY *is*

all that the name implies,

period.

The little gem, here presented,

is destined to make its way in the world.

Under the sponsorship of this charming couple

it will find its reward

(don't peek) ...

at journey's end.

BI-SEXUAL JOHN...

Yes, dear, it can happen to you.

Really.

But just be nonchalant, composed, unperturbed

and fully possessed of equanimity and sang-froid,

if you have the time.

Remember:

all for one

and one for all.

To say nothing of

liberté, egalité,

fraternité.

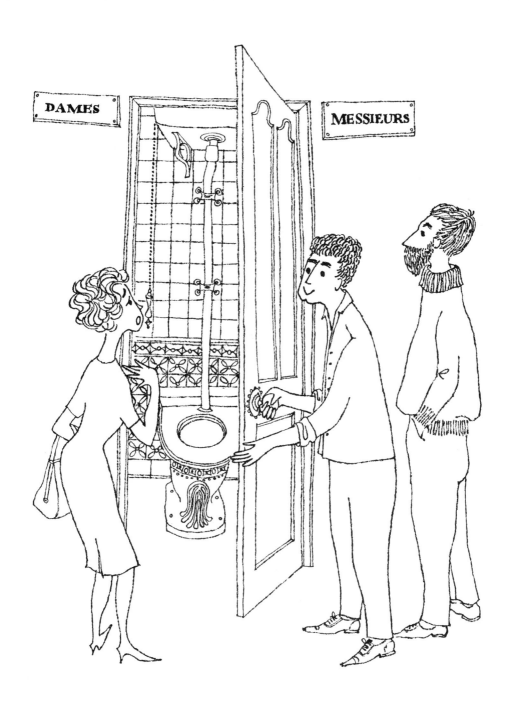

DAMES

MESSIEURS

THE DOUCHE IT YOURSELF...

This neat contrivance,

similar to a French-style phone

(but you talk at it and not into it)

you lift from its cradle

and proceed with a series of calisthenics

designed to give you full coverage

except for what you may inadvertently squirt

over your right

or left

shoulder at your wrist watch

on the bathroom shelf.

LE PAPIER DU JOHNNY...

In general, you'll find three species:

sanded, waxed and newspaper.

The fourth category is your own product if

you take it with you...

or Kleenex, if you're smart.

European innkeepers are aware of the drawbacks

but complaints will get you nowhere.

They are not interested in a soft touch,

blandly maintaining that

mere matter of texture

will not change the travel pattern of nations.

16

THE CUTIE IN THE CORNER...

There are literal-minded

innkeepers who maintain that a room with a shower

means precisely that.

So, here we have one with a doccia right in the corner.

Beautifully located,

it has south and west exposure

with nothing to spoil the view. Not, at least,

for the knock-as-you-enter waiter breaking in

with petit-dejeuner.

THE JOAN OF ARC...

Here you have temperature control

like that offered to Shadrach and associates

in the fiery furnace.

Turn it on CHAUD

(hot)

and it comes out hot.

Turn it on FROID

(cold)

and it comes out

boiling hot.

You're steamed like a plum pudding.

But it can reduce you to ashes which,

much to the annoyance of the femme du chambre,

leaves a ring around the tub.

21

INDOOR OUTHOUSE...

Here we have it,

continental country-house style.

Even in some chateaux,

you must be in the know.

Carry no lantern in the nocturnal hours and

keep the windows closed,

your inclination to the contrary notwithstanding.

Bats,

bees,

and bugs

are very partial to this type of accommodation.

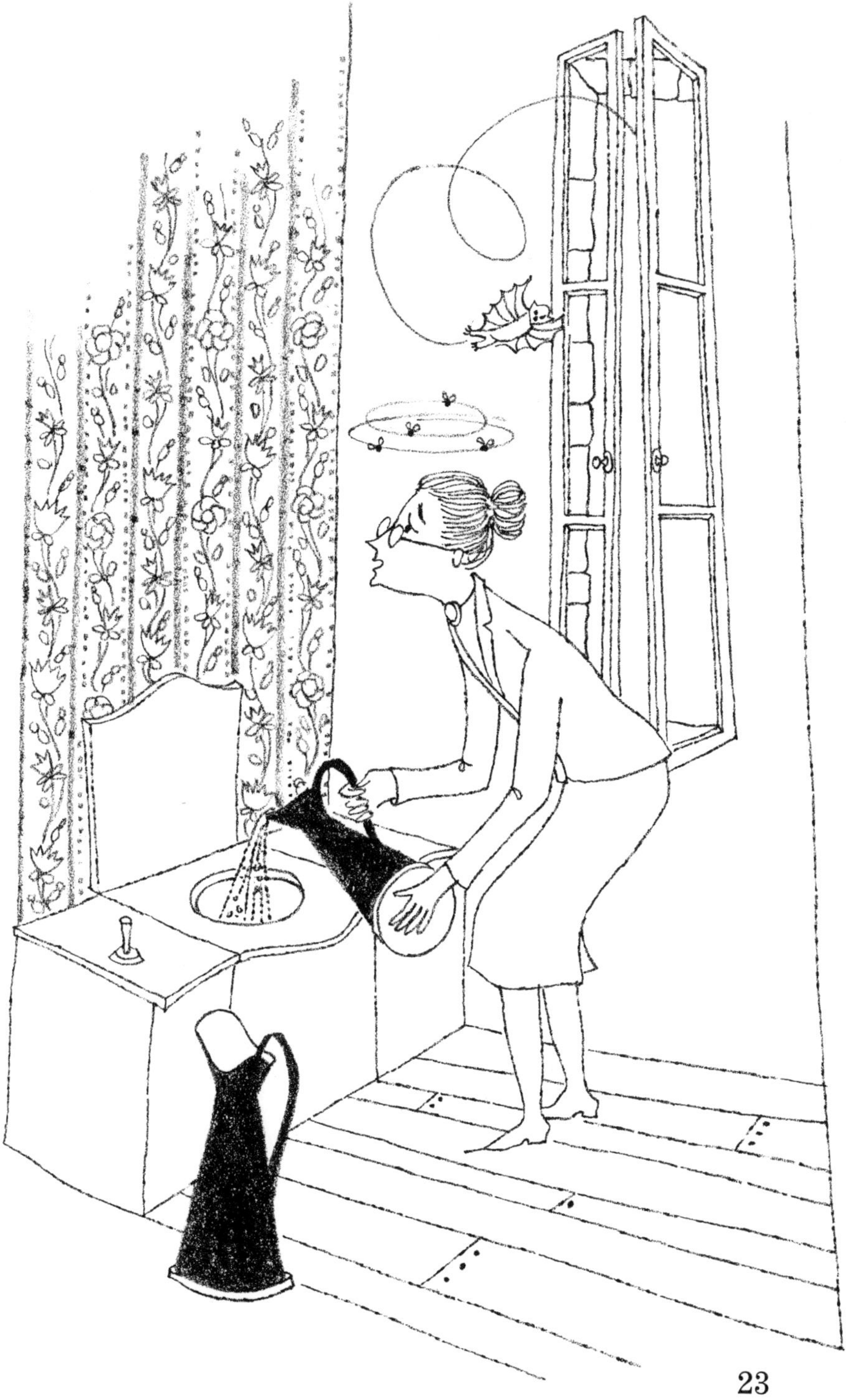

THE KATZENJAMMER...

This type of monkey cage

gives the imprisoned victim

unlimited opportunities for a workout in a limited area.

If you need to be needled

this is your dish.

Make free with the valve handles

and have good clean fun.

A fair measure of the frustrated downpour

and outpour

will finally bring the water on the bathroom floor

to the proper level for Junior to enjoy a good wade.

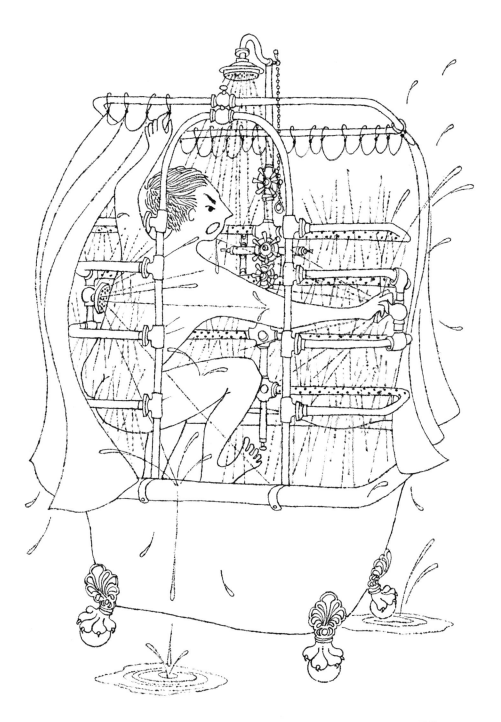

THE SCOTCH MIST...

A more distant cousin than

the aforementioned "Katzenjammer"

with a perforated plug in the ceiling

and making like fine precipitation in the

English Lake Country or the north of Scotland.

This makes a shower curtain unnecessary

but a raincoat or umbrella is advised...

no use getting wet.

27

THE PEDESTRIAN'S PORT OF CALL...

The decorous English would term it an

"outdoor convenience." The very practical French

have their own name for it: pissoir.

And a very practical convenience it is.

Proper courtesies are always observed

as witness this ambidextrous gentleman tipping his hat.

Leave it to the Latins —

no matter how busy they may be,

toujours "noblesse oblige."

THE HOT SEAT...

How do you like yourself...

medium or well-done?

This type of cooking facility

(found in some private homes)

offers several interesting choices.

It's a good idea to fill the tub first

unless you prefer a roast.

In that event, baste yourself well with a good red wine.

And don't forget to turn over

so that you will be properly done on both sides.

Of course most people,

particularly when sober,

just add water

and bring to a boil.

31

THE TURKISH DELIGHT...

is not confined to the Near East.

A simplified form of plumbing...

simplified for the plumber, that is.

Originated during the time of the Ottoman Empire

and probably responsible for

the fall of it.

Your comments

including standing ovations

are, shall we say,

anticipated

but not solicited.

THE STRAIGHT JACKET...

Here you have a real stall shower

even though half the size

of a telephone booth.

The water plays where it may,

but your big problem is

how to retrieve the elusive soap from the shower floor.

Something like diving for a dime in a jam-packed elevator.

Houdini could have done it...

why not you?

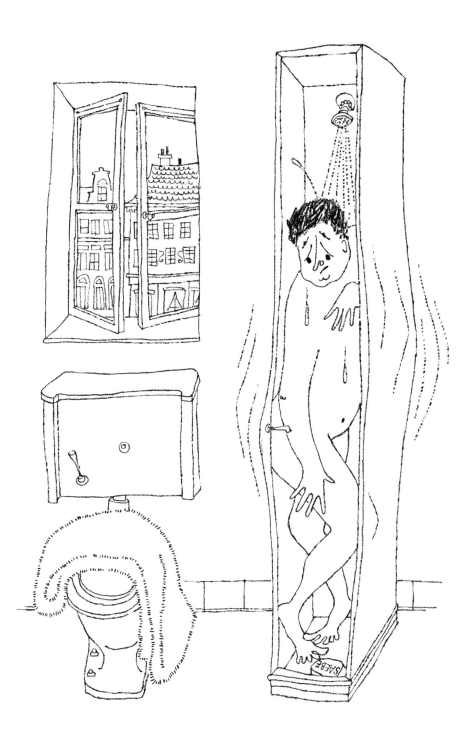

35

THE BIDET*...

Here we present that great enigma

(to most Americans)

of the plumbing world.

First, let us say that not all bidets spray.

Some gurgle;

some flow; some spit; some swirl;

some just fizzle.

No reason for getting all steamed up about the problem.

No cause for puzzlement or frustration.

Let your American resourcefulness come to the fore.

To bidet or not to bidet and the hell with it.

Permit us here to offer some unique

but practical

suggestions

on the following pages...

The Footsie

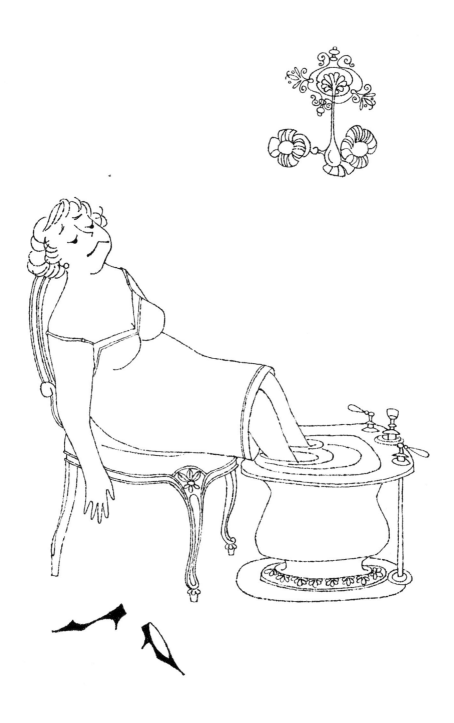

Champagne, anyone?

The Storm

The Aquarium

The Launderette

46

New Development

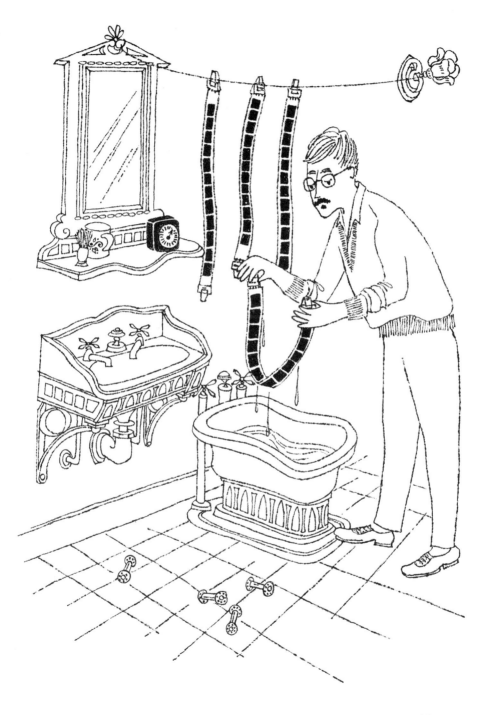

THE CASCADE...

This is a rare and novel type

of devilishly clever contraption.

The shower and tub are so arranged that half the flow

follows a groove in the tub rim and pours

over the edge.

There being no drain in the bathroom floor,

the water level rises while you bathe.

Place your rubbers close at hand

on the bathroom stool

to insure a comfortable exit.

THE LINK TRAINER...

This has a profusion of levers,

knobs,

handles and

buttons (no dials)

obviously intended for only seasoned air pilots

or graduate engineers.

No book of instructions is provided.

Hands off this one unless you have

no fear of death by drowning.

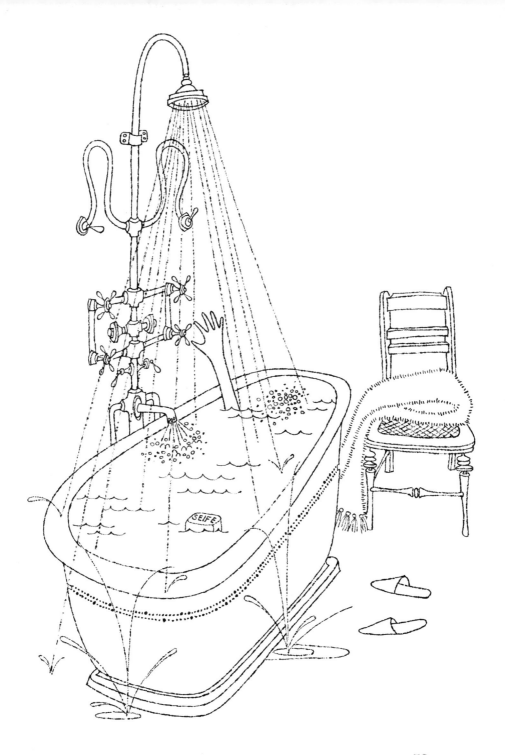

THE SQUARE DEAL...

Only the venturesome

traveller into remote areas of any

continent and the U.K.

may encounter

this four-square seat to the throne.

Good plain construction and no nonsense about it.

Just the thing some playful American tourist

might carry home to frame Uncle Joe's portrait

over the family bar.

In situs, however,

strictly for squares.

THE KNOTHEAD...

This unique shower head is fixed

(and we do mean fixed)

above the head of the tub

and aimed at the toilet

just beyond the foot. Its fire-hose action

is full assurance that the water

will carry the distance

unless baffled by the bather.

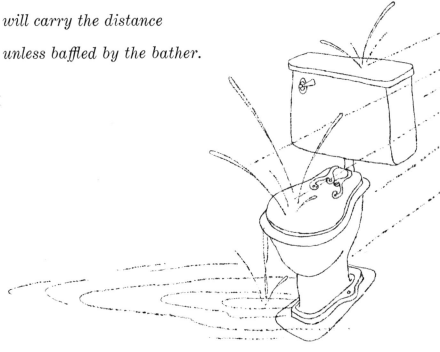

SEIFE

THE ROILED FLUSH(ER)...

This determined lady, dear **observer,**

is neither a bit potty

nor engaged in bathroom **calisthenics.**

Irritated,

frustrated,

but with a grim resolve,

she's merely giving her all to **the** *Empire...or,*

more specifically,

to a bit of its rugged plumbing.

Sort of a chain reaction, so to speak.

But for one in her position,

it's bad luck to break the chain.

THE FINISH IN FINNISH...

The sauna is strictly for the ruggedly individualistic

visitor to Finland who wants to find out

how the other half lives...

and bathes.

In the small steam-filled hut

you work your way up the step-like platforms

beating yourself and your bathmates betimes

with a sturdy birch whisk.

For the grand finale, go out and roll in the snow.

Good, clean masochistic fun all around.

THE DRIP...

The initial rumblings of

this cantankerous contraption

gives promise of great things to come.

But it finally comes

drop

by

drop,

a cross between the old Chinese torture method

and the irritation of

a leaky faucet. However

(like the well-known brand of coffee)

it's good to the

last

drop...

if you can hang around that long.

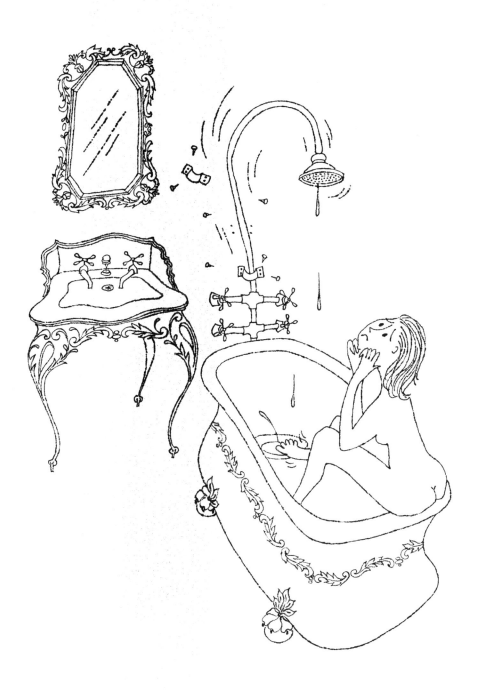

THE TRICKY LAVABO...

Provided with a fabulous faucet,

this brainchild of an inspired plumbing engineer

offers a challenge.

Intercepted at shoulder height, the water runs

up your sleeves.

At the lower levels, you're in for a big

splash.

A little more clearance and you could

stand in the bowl for a shower.

Any way you figure it,

you can't win.

THE DEADHEAD...

This fascinating fixture is peculiar to Majorca

and shrewdly installed by the management

with the desire to have the hostelry rated officially

"De Luxe"...all rooms with shower and bath.

No water pipes are connected but that is

of minor importance. Very few tourists

will take accommodations without private shower or bath.

Be happy that your host has been so

progressive.

THE FALSE ALARM...

The old jingle says, girls,

you may hang your clothes on a hickory limb, etc., etc.

But that doesn't include

the bell-pull over the bath-tub — intended strictly

for use in emergencies

by those in distress.

Hang your damp panties on the cord and you trigger

a gong in the housekeeper's office...

with embarrassing consequences.

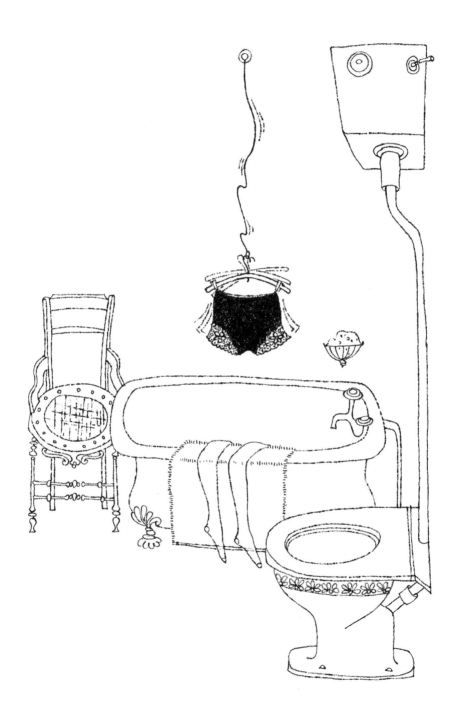

THE RAIN-BIRD...

This ingenious shower

provides a copious flow of water from on high.

It falleth as a gentle rain from heaven

(mostly upon the bathroom floor beneath,

there being no shower curtain).

This problem is wisely resolved, however,

by an open drain in the bathroom floor

which also affords comfortable accommodation

for insect life.

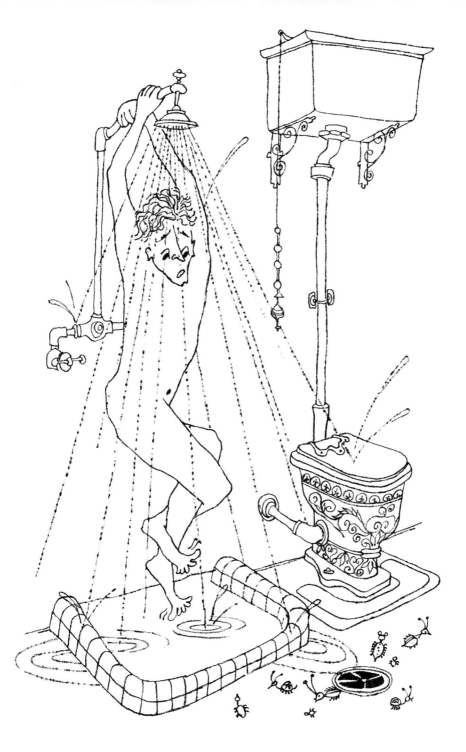

THE TWIN JOHNS...

If they seem a bit chummy,

just remember it's an old

European

custom.

Here you employ the relaxed approach.

If a man answers,

shut up.

You're in the right place, he's

in the right place...

but it's no place for conversation.

73

THE MYSTERY OF THE MISSING MISS...

You may wangle

a bath in certain continental homes

but be prepared for anything

including an exploding gaz heater.

The high tub should be vaulted from a footstool.

Having settled therein, you may find

that it narrows to a point at the bottom

despite the fact that you

don't.

If you can't pry yourself out in due course,

you could be listed as

a missing person.

74

CUMULUS
GAZ

HAPPY ACRES...

In this outsize bath we have

not so much a puzzle in plumbing as

a problem in reaching the desired

objective

in the cavernous interior. Its size makes that

a matter of some consequence.

Close at hand is the Hollywood Bowl...resembling

that California colossus of culture

with respect to its impressive size. For a close

view of yourself in the mirror:

field glasses.

Acres and acres here...and they're all yours.

LE STANDBY, AT JOURNEY'S END...

Our old friends again...remember?

Found now amid these gracious surroundings,

LE STAND-BY *has obviously arrived.*

A life of service

finds its reward in decor-ous *retirement.*

N'est-ce-pas?

78

LONDON

Vienna DUBLIN
ANKARA
MILAN
BORDEAUX

LONDON
NAPLES
TAG
HANOVER
GENEVA

GOTHENBURG
EDINBURGH
ROMA
ROMA
London
NDON
GIBRALTAR
DUBLIN
MADRID
BELGRADE
BARCELONA
ISTANBUL
ROME
AMSTERDAM
STOCKHOLM
ATHENS

INVERNESS
Dusseldorf
BRISTOL
ZURICH
AMSTERDAM
ABERDEEN
NICE

COPENHAGEN
GLASGOW
LONDON
DUBLIN
HAMBURG
PARIS

NICE
Venice
ING

ROME
Stuttgart
LUCERNE
ZURICH